Essentials of 5S Housekeeping

SHYAM BHATAWDEKAR

Dr KALPANA BHATAWDEKAR

Essentials of 5S Housekeeping

Books by Shyam Bhatawdekar and Dr Kalpana Bhatawdekar

1. *HSoftware* (Human Software) (The *Only* Key to Higher Effectiveness)
2. Sensitive Stories of Corporate World (Management Case Studies)
3. Classic Management Games, Exercises, Energizers and Icebreakers (Volume 1)
4. Classic Management Games, Exercises, Energizers and Icebreakers (Volume 2)
5. Stress? No Way!! (Handbook on Stress Management)
6. *HSoftware* (Shyam Bhatawdekar's Effectiveness Model)
7. Competencies and Competency Matrix
8. Essentials of Work Study (Method Study and Work Measurement
9. Essentials of Time Management (Taking Control of Your Life)
10. Essentials of 5S Housekeeping
11. The Romance of Intimacy
12. Good People (Dream of a Boundary Less world)- *Novel*
13. Funny (and Not So Funny) Short Stories
14. Stories Children Will Love (Volume 1: Bhanu-Shanu-Kaju-Biju and Dholu Ram Gadbad Singh)
15. Travelogue: Scandinavia, Russia

To Our Family

Shyam Bhatawdekar   Dr Kalpana Bhatawdekar

"5S Housekeeping" is simple, methodical and effective system of housekeeping. This system was first implemented in Japan. Later it has been adopted all over the world because of its multifarious advantages.

You can implement it not only in factories, offices and stores but also at homes, hospitals and schools. And every individual can do it. The investments to implement "5S" are absolutely minimal and the benefits are enormous. It is also a basic system for launching various other quality systems like TPM, TQM, JIT etc.

Considering its tremendous benefits a thorough knowledge of "5S Housekeeping" becomes imperative. To facilitate gaining the knowledge in this important subject in the shortest possible time, the authors Shyam Bhatawdekar and Dr Kalpana Bhatawdekar included only the "essentials" of "5S" in the book.

The authors are top-notch business executives, highly sought after business and management consultants, eminent management gurus, authentic human behavior experts and prolific authors. And so the book "Essentials of 5S Housekeeping" becomes an authentic document on the subject.

To read more by the authors, refer their websites: http://shyam.bhatawdekar.com, *http://writings-of-shyam.blogspot.com* and http://management-universe.blogspot.com

Essentials of 5S Housekeeping

Shyam Bhatawdekar
Dr Kalpana Bhatawdekar

Published by Publishing Division of

Prodcons Group

8, Pranjal Society, Shiv Tirth Nagar, Paud Road, Pune 411038 (India)

Email: prodcons@prodcons.com

For other web publications, refer: http://management-universe.blogspot.com and http://shyam.bhatawdekar.com

Copyright © with the authors Shyam Bhatawdekar and Dr Kalpana Bhatawdekar

All rights reserved

No reproduction without permission in whole or in part in any form

Contents

1. 5S Housekeeping Is Fundamental
2. 5S Housekeeping: A Glance
3. Vision
4. Advantages
5. Elements of 5S
6. Steps to Implement the 5 Elements of 5S
7. Consequences of Not Practicing 5S
8. Five Levels of 5S Housekeeping
9. Stages of 5S Housekeeping
10. Steps and Critical Factors in implementing 5S
11. Implementation Methodology
12. 5S Pledge
13. Criteria for Good Housekeeping Award
14. 5S Audits
15. What Practitioners Say about 5S Housekeeping
16. Be Tidy and Reclaim One Third of Your Life
17. 5S Housekeeping at Home

Essentials of 5S Housekeeping

5S Housekeeping Is Fundamental

- 5S Housekeeping is fundamental for enhancing the value for the customer.
- 5S Housekeeping is the foundation for all the organizational systems/processes, which in turn, enhance value to customers.

5S Housekeeping: A Glance

- Started as Japanese concept of workplace upkeep and improvement.
- Since early 80's in Japan and later picked up all over the world.
- Pioneer- Toyota, Japan.
- Systematic approach to good housekeeping.
- People oriented approach: every individual can contribute to improve his workplace.
- Participative approach: every individual can take part in it.

- Practice oriented approach: cleaner, better, effective, productive and safer workplace.
- 5S stands for the five good housekeeping principles each principle starting with alphabet "S".

Vision

- To keep one's external and internal house in order, develop sensitivity for one's surroundings and a concern for the environment at large.
- A systematic and rational approach to workplace organization and methodical housekeeping with a sense of purpose.

Advantages

- Workplace becomes cleaner and better organized.
- Shop floor and office operations become easier and safer.
- Results are visible to everyone- insiders and outsiders.
- Problems detected fast.

- Visibility gives rise to further improvements. Increased number of suggestions.
- People are disciplined.
- It instills pride among people.
- Happier employees with high morale and greater employee involvement.
- Better use of floor space.
- Less work in progress and inventories.
- Less time in material handling.
- Retrieval time minimized.
- Better flow of work.
- More time for improvement activities.
- Low machine breakdown rate. Low down time. Better preventive maintenance.
- Low accident rate.
- High yield of materials.
- High and consistent product quality.
- Low overall cost.
- Higher value for money to customers.
- Better aesthetics.
- Company image enhances and generates more business.

Elements of 5S

5S encompasses 5 simple steps:

1. *Seiri:* Sorting out. Remove unnecessary items as appropriate. Keep what is necessary.
2. *Seiton:* Systematic arrangement. Prefix or decide a place for everything and put everything in place so that it can be accessed and retrieved easily and efficiently.
3. *Seiso:* Spic and span. Shine. Cleaning not for beautification alone but with a sense of purpose. No dust. No dirt. Systematic cleaning.
4. *Seiketsu:* Standardization. Develop standards and evaluation criteria. Standardize the operating procedures (SOPs) for cleaning. Serene atmosphere and sanitizing. Environmental cleanliness.
5. *Shitsuke:* Self-discipline/training. Create awareness of first 4S's and train to implement and sustain.

You must have noticed that each element of 5S Housekeeping starts with the alphabet "S". So you have five Japanese words for the five elements each one starting with "S" giving this system its name "5S Housekeeping".

Steps to Implement the 5 Elements of 5S

1. Seiri

- Classification- sort out. Identify necessary and unnecessary items.
- Elimination- remove unnecessary items as appropriate.
- Storage keeping in mind:
    - Frequent use/rare use items.
    - Close location/distant location
    - Identification of items
- Fix responsibilities and share responsibilities.
- Monitor progress.

Rough Criteria for Seiri

- Items not used for a year- check and throw.
- Used only once in last 6 to 12 months- store at a distance.
- Used only once in last 1 to 6 months- store at a central place in the work area.
- Used weekly/hourly/daily- store near work site.

Seiri: Obstacles

Seiri is not as easy to practice, as it seems because of the following thinking:

- It is wasteful to throw things away.
- We might possibly use them later.
- It was so much trouble for me to make these things.
- I know it is not used but it is in good condition, let it be there.
- I want every thing here. I may use these any time, I can't tell when. So don't remove anything.

If you think it is "such a waste to throw it away", you can't get started.

2. Seiton

- Ensure rational layout of machines, equipment, cabinets etc.
- Place frequently used items at the point of use.
- Prefix or decide a place for everything and put everything in its place.
- Use labels, color codes to identify.

- Use index for files, records and drawings.
- Plan storage with easy retrievability.
- Mixed-up items in cabinets should be organized.
- Make cabinets, shelves, racks self-explanatory through identification aids.
- Have visual controls for checking missing items.

3. *Seiso*

- Develop standards of cleaning.
- Clean up work place, machines and tools after use.
- Clean up supply line (no leakage, blockage, clogging with oil/dirt).
- Assign responsibilities and schedules for cleaning.
- Clean waste bins at end of shift/day.
- Clean light bulbs, fans, shades, reflectors etc.
- Pay special attention to scrap yard, gardens, godowns etc.
- Scrap and chips from machines could fall directly in to collecting bins.

4. *Seiketsu*

- Identify 5S areas.

- Develop standards/evaluation criteria with workmen (SOPs and housekeeping standards).
- Establish checking procedure 5W + 1H.
- Establish feedback procedure 5W + 1H.
- Wear neat and clean uniform.
- Wear protective clothing.
- Provide adequate lighting, ventilation, exhaust etc.
- Check electrical wiring, cables, switches etc.
- Maintain sanitary/hygienic conditions in washrooms, locker rooms, canteen and kitchen.
- Earmark smoking and eating areas.
- Look for heavy noise, vibrations and heat in machines, analyze for root cause and take action.
- Create visual control systems.
- Devise ways to expose hidden problems.
- Create standards.

5. *Shitsuke*

- Create awareness of first 4 S's.
- Develop action details for maintaining standards.
- Make them easily understandable.
- Give specific directions.

- Display correct work procedure on the floor.
- Correct deviations on the spot.
- Maintain punctuality.
- Conduct audits.
- Demonstrate sincerity in following rules.
- Share success to enthuse others.

Consequences of Not Practicing 5S

Seiri

- The unwanted clutters up the place and the wanted is hard to find.
- More time spent for searching things.
- More space required.
- We can't bring in new things in the same place.
- Causes wrong identification and rejected parts are moved to work station.

Seiton

- Things are seldom available when needed. More time spent for locating misplaced things.

- Defective and good items/similar looking items get mixed-up.
- Items are lost.
- Prone to accidents.
- Loss of production.
- Excess inventory.
- Pressure for more space and storage equipment.

Seiso

- Dust and dirt will affect the machine performance and process capabilities.
- Cleaning reveals hidden problems, which may get overlooked otherwise.
- Dust and dirt affect performance and aesthetic quality.
- Unpleasant work place.

Five Levels of 5S Housekeeping

- Housekeeping of one's inner self.
- Following the 5S principles and reducing waste.
- Extending the 5S concepts to include ergonomics.

- Extending the 5S concepts to include aesthetics.
- Maintaining records and educating others.

Stages of 5S Housekeeping

Stage 1: Floor is full of unwanted material.
Stage 2: Clutter found by the walls.
Stage 3: Factory/office is clean but tools, papers, files and materials dis-organized.
Stage 4: Storage area/offices are clean and furniture, documents, material organized.
Stage 5: Factory/office is immaculate.

Steps and Critical Factors in Implementing 5S

- Top /Senior Management commitment.
- Leadership by location heads.
- Awareness training programs for all employees.
- Launching of 5S program.
- Allocation of funds.
- Identification on 5S areas.
- Team formation involving employees.
- Developing standards.

- Developing checklists.
- Guidance, training, sorting out problems.
- Developing audit check lists.
- Publishing audit results.
- Reviewing audit findings, follow up corrective actions.
- Holding competitions- awards.

Implementation Methodology

- All employees to undergo 5S Housekeeping training.
- A vision statement to be evolved and started with all employees.
- Divide the organization into convenient zones.
- Divide each zone in to convenient sub-zones.
- Decide on date(s) for launching 5S in each zone, sub-zone.
- Take pledge (refer the section titled "5S Pledge" for couple of formats of the pledge as examples. They can be customized to your requirements).
- Apply 5S principles step by step.
- Form audit teams.

- Carry out audits.

5S Pledge

Examples of Pledge Formats:

Example 1: It shall be my (our) constant effort to maintain my workplace in an excellent order by sorting out unwanted material periodically and discarding them, assigning a place for everything and keeping everything in its place and keeping my workplace neat and clean all the time everyday.

Example 2: It shall be my (our) endeavor to delight our customers (or internal and external customers) by adhering to the standards of putting things in order and maintaining cleanliness at our workplace.

Criteria for Good Housekeeping Award

- Space occupied.
- Ease of retrieval.
- Ingenious storing methods.

- Waste elimination.
- Aesthetics.

5S Audits

- Form an audit team for each zone consisting of 4-5 members. The members should belong to that zone. One member may belong to another zone so as to maintain impartiality.
- Auditing should be carried out once a month or once in two months based on a carefully prepared checklist.

An Example of Auditor's Checklist

- Documents maintained as per retention plan: 10 points.
- Other items at assigned places: 10 points.
- Innovative methods of storage/visual display system: 5 points.
- Cleanliness/hygiene: 5 points.
- Space released: 5 points.
- Reporting of waste reduction: 5 points.

- Aesthetic aspect: 10 points.
- Safety aspect: 15 points.
- Auditee's personal appearance: 5 points.
- Layout: 5 points.
- Lighting level: 5 points.
- Noise level: 5 points.
- Temperature/humidity: 5 points.
- General ergonomics: 10 points.

What Practitioners Say about 5S Housekeeping

- 5S Housekeeping is literally the workplace management.
- It is pre-requisite for world class manufacturing practices.
- It is an ideal housekeeping system and beyond.
- 5S is doing away with unwanted things and waste reduction.
- 5S Housekeeping is keeping things in their respective places without any one's supervision.
- It paves way for almost zero retrieval time situations.
- It is keeping the workplace spic and span.

- It is keen inspection.
- 5S is about adopting standards for sustenance.
- It provides for good service practices.
- It is a habit and not just a one time or intermittent action.
- It is an attitude and not an audit or policing.
- In a way 5S should become the work culture.
- It promotes safety of high order.
- It adds confidence.
- It subtracts pain.
- It multiplies productivity.
- It divides pleasure among all.
- It enhances participation.
- It builds team spirit and strengthens teamwork.
- It brings out creativity of the people and their contribution.
- It improves motivation and morale of the people.
- It provides foundation for implementing other quality systems like TPM, TQM, JIT etc.
- It increases the value (for money) to the customers.
- It is a very well thought out system- very simple to understand and implement and yet very potent.

Be Tidy and Reclaim One Third of Your Life

Most people must be wondering as to how one can get back so many lost years of one's life for better use. We have done some work out for you. Read:

Suppose you live for 90 years (We pray that you should live forever. We took 90 years life span merely for ease of calculations).

Of 90 years, one uses about 8 hours per day in sleeping (and that you must do for good health). So, you spend approximately one third of your entire life in sleeping i.e. 30 years.

Left with you are: 60 years when you are awake.

Now recall your every day routine from the time you wake up till you go to sleep. It is full of one activity i.e. **searching.** Searching everything- searching toothbrush, towel, clothes, shoes, spectacles, vehicle keys, office keys, identity card, papers, data, information, files, telephone numbers and hundreds of other things.

Researches have shown that on an average, an OK (or so-so) tidy and lukewarmly disorganized person (not the real tidy and organized person) wastes some 30% of his available waking time in searching all kinds of things because he cannot find things in place and takes lots of time locating and retrieving them. You will agree that a large number of people come in this category.

So 30% of available 60 years of life go in air without really being put to any good use (searching things is definitely not a good use of time). That's precious some 20 years of life.

Imagine losing big 20 years of life in a non-value adding activity called searching because of not being tidy and organized.

Lesson: Get tidy. Get organized- *place for everything and everything in place* and recover your otherwise lost 20 long years of life for doing more purposeful activities.

Good luck!!

The next section of the book deals with application of 5S Housekeeping at homes.

5S Housekeeping at Home

5S- Five Steps to Prosperity and Success for Your Home

1. SEIRI (Sort out and dispose)

Eliminate unnecessary things. Keep only what is needed. Undertake major cleaning. Save money on buying unnecessary additional storage equipment and space.

2. SEITON (Place for everything and everything in place)

Establish a neat layout to fix storage places and the methods and stick to the rules. Eliminate search time and therefore, stresses and strains. Save money by not purchasing the items now easily available at home.

3. SEISO (Scrub, dusting and cleaning)

Understanding that cleanliness is a form of inspection. Establish state of cleanliness commensurate to your needs. Involve every family member. Achieve zero grime and zero dirt. Give a definite time each day for cleaning.

4. SEIKETSU (standardize the methods of 5S and environmental upkeep)

Establish standards for maintaining. Add color and use innovative visible management so that abnormalities show up for early action. Also make sure that you contribute to environmental upkeep.

5. SHITSUKE (Self discipline and training)

Feeling accountable and setting examples to maintain the established procedures of orderliness and neatness. Full participation in developing and practicing good habits.

Do you find following things within fifteen to twenty seconds after they are needed?

- A particular medicine: say antacid tablets, painkillers, your daily medicines doctor prescribed, sprain cream etc.
- Postage and related material: say stamps, envelops, inland letters, post cards, glue, gem clips, stapler, staple pins, stationery etc.
- Bank documents; like pay-in-slips, check books etc.

- Income tax related documents like papers related to your investments, previous years' income tax returns etc.
- Electricity/power bills, telephone bills, water bills, corporation tax bills etc.
- Telephone numbers and addresses of your particular relative or friend or your or your spouse's particular colleague.
- Writing pad and pen/pencil to take down the messages over the telephone.
- Your cell phones.
- Locks and keys of your house, scooters, car(s), cupboards, safe deposit lockers, office, keys and locks of your suitcases, brief cases etc.
- Desired pair of shoes/footwear, matching clothes, hairpins, kerchief, nail polish, lipstick etc.
- Children's school bag, books, notebooks, their shoes/footwear, socks, progress cards, i-cards, date of birth certificate, their particular toys, ink bottles, pens, pencils etc.
- The stitching kit like pairs of scissors, sewing needles, threads of particular colors and types, buttons of various types, measuring tape, knives etc.
- Towels, toothpaste, toothbrushes, soaps, detergents.

- Candles and match box when the light/power goes off suddenly.
- The tong, the gas lighter, the hand mixer, right kind of serving bowls, right kind of cutlery, cups and saucers.
- The cooking recipes you so diligently took down from a TV program or copied from a magazine or web site.
- A particular novel or book/magazine you wish to read today, now.
- Your housecoat when suddenly some guests arrive and you have to receive them at your door.
- The money or change you kept somewhere.
- Your or your spouse's i-cards, credit cards, pass ports, club membership cards etc.
- Shoe polish of various colors and types, shoe brushes, shoelaces etc.

If your answers to many of these questions and such other possible questions are in negative or you have hesitation in answering them, you have large scope of improving your housekeeping following the above mentioned 5S Housekeeping steps.

Did Any of the Following Things Happen at Your Home at Least Once in the Past Six Months or One Year?

- Your kitchen or other rooms of the house got flooded with water since somebody in the house kept the taps open.
- Electricity/power bill suddenly shot up during some months because the family members are not in the habit of switching off the air-conditioners, heaters, lights, fans, geysers/boilers, ovens, computers and other electrical appliances when not in use.
- The sauce/ketchup, pickles, jam, shampoo, oil bottles' caps were not securely placed and so got dropped and broke and the contents were wasted.
- The computer, printer, mixer, fans, clocks/watches etc stopped working suddenly as too much of dirt and dust jammed the inside of these machines and you had to pay heavily to get them rectified that too not to your satisfaction or you had to buy the new ones with lots of extra expenditure not planned.
- You had to buy an additional cupboard (storage space) or two to store the things because the existing storage space had fully been utilized.

- You found cockroaches and spiders etc many times in your utensils, cups and saucers and in many others items at your home.
- You or any other member(s) of the family was injured by the shaving blade which was used up but not disposed off and was rusted.
- Did you find rusted hair clips, rusted safety pins lying on the washbasins of your home and the rust spoiling the washbasin and also the possibility of using these rusted items by you or the members of your family?
- Your bathroom was not dry and was slippery and as a result some one slipped off, fell down and got injured or got electric shock due to wet floor (if he/she was an old person, it can be very dangerous).

If your answers to many of these questions is in affirmation, you need to consider giving 5S Housekeeping a high priority for your home.

Discuss among your family members the need for implementing 5S Housekeeping, let them understand the system and then with their participation implement it. The results will please everyone at home.

More on SEITON- Place for everything and everything in place

A large number of homemakers wish to be efficient. And they should be, why not? They wish to hurry up everything because of lack of time and compulsions of punctuality for every activity.

Then, for accomplishing it, they take out everything that is needed to finish up that job within the time available. For example, take cooking. You have pressure on you of completing the cooking in time since you, you spouse and children have to start for their workplaces on time. You pick out from the cupboards all the needed utensils, all the gadgets, all the raw materials and spread all of them around you, all at a time on your kitchen platform and kitchen island thinking that placing everything around you would allow you easy access to them. But the very clutter around you really becomes an obstacle in efficient working. Plus, you are compromising on safety due to the clutter. It looks untidy and loses aesthetics.

After the cooking is complete, you find that there are hundred things on your kitchen platform and kitchen island now and you just do not have time and energy to put these things back in the places meant for them. It's time up for you. You and everyone else in the family have to rush out to accomplish the next tasks ahead. So, you leave the kitchen in this kind of unorganized condition. Then, in the evening, you start from where you left, take out some more things to do the evening's cooking and the clutter keeps mounting. The whole of kitchen starts looking untidy. The retrieval is difficult and time consuming. It's unsafe.

Rather than doing this, plan out your cooking sequence. Take out one thing at a time from the cupboards that are just a step away from you in the kitchen; they are not far away from you. After you have used that thing, put it back in the cupboard in its place immediately. The time taken to use that item is the same- you are not taking any extra time or losing any time. You are as efficient.

Do this for each item of use. Take it out, use it and place it back in the same condition in which you took it (if there was a lid on bottle, place it back securely) and position it in the same place from where you took it out. Thus the things always remain in their designated places all the time and the house looks well organized and tidy.

You will take same amount of time and there would not be any clutter around. The kitchen will look tidy and will be a safe place to work.

Give it a try.

Benefits of Adopting 5S Housekeeping at Home

- Home looks clean, tidy and beautiful.
- Feels great to live in such a home.
- Impresses everyone.
- Improves hygiene at home.
- No one at home wastes any time in searching and retrieving the things. Please read an earlier write-up in this book on how to save twenty year of your life.
- Home is a safe place now.
- The environment around is clean and healthy.
- There is no clutter around.
- You don't need to spend money to procure additional storage space or equipment for that clutter (had you not done the 5S Housekeeping, the clutter would have increased). So, you are saving lots of money. (For saving money, read more tips at URL: http://save-money-ideas.blogspot.com/)

- You will experience more and more surprising advantages as you start implementing 5S Housekeeping at home.

www.ingramcontent.com/pod-product-compliance
Lightning Source LLC
Chambersburg PA
CBHW061521180526
45171CB00001B/280